T0132009

The Girl Who Grew Up Saving Animals

Karen Burnett

AuthorHouse™ UK
1663 Liberty Drive
Bloomington, IN 47403 USA
www.authorhouse.co.uk
UK TFN: 0800 0148641 (Toll Free inside the UK)
UK Local: 02036 956322 (+44 20 3695 6322 from outside the UK)

Because of the dynamic nature of the Internet, any web addresses or links contained in this book may have changed since publication and may no longer be valid. The views expressed in this work are solely those of the author and do not necessarily reflect the views of the publisher, and the publisher hereby disclaims any responsibility for them.

This book is printed on acid-free paper.

ISBN: 978-1-6655-9170-6 (sc)
ISBN: 978-1-6655-9171-3 (e)

Print information available on the last page.

Published by AuthorHouse 07/27/2021

authorHOUSE®

Contents

Acknowledgements

I wish to acknowledge the following people:

- Frances Kavanagh for taking the time to type the manuscript and edit photos;
- Marie Lusher from whom I got two handsome dogs, Sky and Mork. Thank you to Marie for the many years of companionship they have given me;
- Faith Worthington, who gave me a dog name Sonny who is still going strong and the many years of friendship we have built as a result;
- Cindi Regan, who has inspired me to do what I love: rescuing animals. Cindi rescues dogs globally from countries including China and Spain. She is a great inspiration. Thank you, Cindi, for giving me the gentle push I needed to get set up.

I dedicate this book to all aforementioned and to the following: my four sons, Matthew, James, Nick, and Dave, and to Emily Pearce and her children, Nuala, Mia, and Denny.

Thank you to Janet Maria Adams, who is like a sister to me and has supported me through some tough times. She has always done a good job of grooming my dogs before shows. These dogs were always placed in the classes they were entered. Thank you for all your help.

I wish to extend this acknowledgement to my good friend Kay Stack, who has been there to look after my pets in cases of emergency, Laura Skelly, who has provided me with help while I undertook my dog grooming course, and Ken Fitzpatrick, who has helped me through some very tough times and loves animals as much as I do. I am very lucky to have such good friends.

Introduction

This book has been written to show how I grew up to love animals and respect them. I hope to inspire children to love animals and not abuse them. This book also shows the cruelty some people inflict upon animals. It will give readers insight into how animals, after they have been treated so cruelly, can benefit when they get rescued. They can turn their lives around and give unconditional love over the years.

This book is a true reflection of my life and career in animal welfare and rescuing and how I chose to work in animal welfare. I hope readers will take this wealth of information and enjoy reading it.

All of the names mentioned are real, and I have received their full permission to use their names.

I have over forty years in animal welfare. During this time, I have rescued thousands of dogs and cats from cruelty and over 30,000 hens over five years in my own rescue. I hope this book will help open the eyes of the young and old alike. If a reader can save the life of the life of just one animal, writing this book will have been worth it.

How It All Began

During school holidays, I worked on four farms (two dairy and two pig farms) to earn my pocket money. Each Wednesday, the farmers would take me with them to the livestock market in Bury St Edmunds. I used to cry as I watched the livestock lorries pull into the yards and unload the animals they had onboard. The handlers used to whip the cows, pigs, and sheep on their rear to make them come out of the lorries. I told myself this was cruel and promised myself at this tender age of seven that after I left school, animal welfare was going to be my career.

I witnessed so much cruelty to animals during my school years. I began to take animals home, and my mother would be mad with me. As time went on, my mother decided, as I continued to bring animals home, I was out of control. So she sent me to boarding school to stop me. This did not stop me as I carried on bringing animals home. My mother contacted the school to ask if I could take some to school and look after them. The school agreed and informed my mother that there was no stopping me as I love animals too much and would work with animals.

At the age of 11, I started to work in a boarding kennel and cattery as they had previously said they would not take me until the age of 11. I was surprised when I saw the conditions where the animals were boarded; that really opened my eyes. I wondered how they could treat other people's animals this way.

My Life as a Rescuer

My life as an animal rescuer has been an eye-opener. When you first see a case of cruelty, you think there cannot be worse, but unfortunately there is. Seeing an animal who is skin and bone, badly malnourished, or dead, you hope you will never have to witness this again. Every case is different, and in some cases, you catch the culprit; in other cases, you don't. For those who are caught, appear in court, and are prosecuted, a rescuer feels a joy of satisfaction and a job well done. There are cases where you think the animals will pull through and surprisingly they do begin to gain weight. These are what I call the real fighters. There are cases where you will receive a report about an animal being ill-treated, and when you attend the call and see a fit and healthy animal, you breathe a sigh of relief.

I wish all calls were like this, but sadly, there will be cases where an animal will need to be taken into care. While some owners are happy to sign the animal over, there are owners who will become abusive and nasty, requiring a call to the police. I have seen some horrific cases of cruelty. Nothing could have prepared me for my first observance of cruelty, when I saw three cats that had been locked in a cellar with no windows or any daylight. They were surrounded by their own urine and faeces. Needless to say, the owners were prosecuted and received the same sentence as the owners of the puppy farm.

Choosing to go into animal welfare is not for the faint-hearted, and in some cases, you will need to have a strong stomach. You will receive reports about animals that have been tied with a heavy chain or beaten and starved. At the age of 15, I worked in a chicken hatchery and sadly watched a person sexing the chicks; the male chicks were gassed. I could not believe when I saw chicks with two heads and three legs. The female chicks were put into boxes with 25 chicks per corner and sent to China.

I officially got involved in animal welfare at the age of 16 as the law required. That is when I decided I wanted to get involved in animal welfare. I have adopted many animals, including some that passed away.

In 2010, I moved to Ireland and started transporting rescued dogs all around the country. I was given a gentle push by my friend Cindi McNeil Regan to start my own rescue. Cindi was a fellow rescuer who at the time was rescuing dogs in Ireland and has since become involved in rescuing dogs globally. I set up my own rescue in 2011, and over a period of five years, I had rescued over four hundred dogs. Cindi was the inspiration and partly responsible for the rescue person I became. I was only able to rescue on a small scale as I was renting a farm and some of the outbuildings were not suitable. During this time, I also began rescuing ex-commercial hens single-handedly.

My Animals and Their Story, One by One

Through the years, I have provided a home to many animals and birds. Some were rescued. I cared for and tended to their needs as they arose.

At the aged of two, I got my first dog, a Jack Russell called Scamp. He lived to be 16 years old.

At age seven, we had two Irish red setters called Rufus and Ruby, a breeding pair requiring high maintenance as regards walking and daily grooming.

At age ten, I had two white rabbits called Whiskey and Snowball, who died at ten years. I also had a cat we called Sweep, who died at 12 years of age.

At age 17, I had a black cat called Zorba and two budgerigars, Bluey and Bindy. Bluey died aged 20, and Bindy at 18.

At age 24, I had a cat named Cindy, who I hand-reared with her three siblings following the death of their mother in labour. Cindy lived for 18 years.

At age 29, I had a black Labrador called Bruno; a rough collie, otherwise known as a Lassie dog, called Bonnie; and a Rottweiler pup called Alies. Bonnie died just before her 18th birthday, and Afie died at age 16. I also had two Rottweiler cross rough collies called Bruno and Donna, which were both black and sandy colour. Donna was a good house dog. They both died at the age of 15.

Mollie was my first border collie, a red and white marl who loved ice cream. Mollie spent her first seven years in and out of rescues before I adopted her. Mollie's teeth had been filed down by a previous owner. Mollie loved her daily ice cream, and on a day when there was none, Mollie would react by throwing her food dish around the kitchen and up the stairs. I had Mollie for 11 years; she died at 18 from cancer.

Crispin, a springer spaniel I got as a pup from Marie Lusher, died at the age of 14.5 from cancer. Mork is a Serbian husky cross I also got from Marie at ten weeks old. Mork will be 14 in July. He won confidents dog of the year when he was only 18 months. He has taken part in agility and entered dog shows in which he has always placed. Mork is a therapy dog in Ireland and England.

Jess, a collie who was rescued from a puppy farm, was also in agility and a show dog as an adult. She died three days before her 18th birthday. She is very much missed.

Sonny is a Siberian husky I rescued from north Wales. He attended a few dog shows before moving to Ireland. Sonny will be 12 years old this year.

Gillie, a pointer cross spaniel, was rescued from death row at just four months old. Gillie is a loving and good house dog but can be temperamental at times.

Ben was an Alaskan malamute in black and white colours with brown eyes I rescued from the death row in the UK. He was subsequently stolen from Thetford in Norfolk. Ben would be ten years old, and he is very much missed.

Tess is a collie cross Labrador. She is black and white and an affectionate six-year-old I rescued from a farm.

Bess is a 15-year-old miniature collie and affectionate dog who loves to bark. Bess tries to be top dog sometimes and causes arguments with her fellow pets, but nothing too serious.

Demon was a black and white Siberian husky with ice-blue eyes who sadly passed away at the age of four from liver cancer. Demon had been left outdoors 24/7 in a yard, was unvaccinated, and was used as a breeding dog before I stepped in.

Suki was a Siamese cat I rescued; she was shy and rarely came out. Suki died at age of 12. She had tested positive for feline AIDS prior to me rescuing her.

Tiny was a loving rescue cat who went out one day and got run over while wandering. Skyla is a pure-white cat with green eyes, and Tiddles and Tibby are sisters. Picasso is a black and white cat; Issac is a ginger tom who loves to hide. Kiara, a sister to Issac, is a black and ginger fleck who also loves to hide. All of the cats are very loving. Flash was a black and white tabby who suddenly died from massive heart attack. She passed away in my arms before the age of three. Tiger Tim was her brother. He unfortunately passed away 11 months after Flash from a blocked bladder. He had shown no signs of illness. I became aware when he had moved from his sleeping place to the litter box. I immediately called the vet as he was unable to stand. Tiger Tim was admitted to a veterinary hospital, where he received treatment to unblock his bladder, but sadly, he passed away 24 hours later. Tom was a ginger cat I only had for a short time as he was killed by a dog at eight months old.

Hen Rescue

During my time as a hen rescuer, I single-handedly rescued and rehomed almost 30,000 birds. I had 150 hens left. Search for Laois Hen Rescue on Google. I have been featured on Irish TV programs and have been featured in articles in the *Laois Nationalist, Leinster Express,* and *Irish Sun* newspapers. Hens, once fully rehabilitated, can survive for five to ten years if you follow the advice, and by law, you should have a registered flock number whether you have one hen and rooster or 101. Regulations state if you do not obtain a flock number, this can result in a fine. Remember if you have hens and ducks, they must be kept separate.

I have enjoyed my years rescuing hens, and if my health will allow, I would love to obtain a new suitable place to do so again.

As a responsible rescuer, I ensured all of the dogs I rescued were vaccinated, microchipped, and neutered. All of the animals who have passed away I very sadly miss.

Are You Considering Getting a Puppy?

Before you commit to getting a puppy, maybe because you think they are cute or a lovely bundle of fluff, ask yourself the following questions:

- Am I prepared to train the dog to walk on a lead?
- Am I prepared for the cleaning following the peeing and pooing overnight?
- Am I prepared for the chewing and damage a puppy may do?
- Am I prepared to crate train the puppy? This does not mean leaving the pup in a crate 24/7. This means training the pup to go into its own space. It should not mean using it for punishment.

If you do decide to get a puppy, remember to choose a breed which will not outgrow your home or garden. Do your homework and research regarding breeds, temperament, size, etc. There are often cases where owners do not do research before they get a dog. Unfortunately some dogs end up being surrendered to the pound or rescues for many of the reasons mentioned above. If you do surrender your dog to the pound, in some cases, they may not have to do their five to seven days in the pound and are unfortunately put to sleep. Please think seriously before surrendering your dog.

What Size or Breed of Dog Do You Want?

Whether you consider purchasing a dog from a registered breeder or a visit to the local dog pound, you should first consider the size of your house and garden and how active you are.

If you live in *a small house or apartment, you should consider a small dog* that will be happy to sit on your lap, go for a walk, and let out in the garden or outdoor area.

If you have a medium-size house and reasonable-size garden, this will be suitable for *a small to medium dog.* A medium dog will need more food and exercise, and depending on hair length, it may need regular grooming. Brushing daily will help get rid of loose hairs, but professional grooming is advisable every couple of months.

If you live in a large house with an extensive garden, you can choose *any size of dog.* It is important to remember large dog breeds, such as Great Danes, St Bernards, and mastiffs, will be more active and will require a lot of food, exercise, and grooming.

Consider the cost. Do you have the finances to keep the dog you choose? Remember your dog will require annual vaccinations, and there may be unexpected vet bills. Consider pet insurance; it can be worthwhile to shop around.

All dogs will require walking and playtime, even what is known as a lapdog. Small dogs have a tendency to yap. Dogs don't like to be left alone for long periods. They like companionship.

Dog Breeds

The following will help you distinguish among breeds, sizing, and suitability.

- **small breeds (from 7 to 35 pounds)**
  Jack Russells, Yorkshire terriers, terriers, long-hair Lhasa apsos, Chinese cresteds (ideal for people who may have allergies to dog hair), bichon frises, Cavalier King Charles spaniels, Scottish terriers, toy poodles, and miniature poodles (ideal for people who may be allergic to dogs).

- **medium breeds (from 35 to 65 pounds)**
  Springer spaniels, water spaniels, collies, beagles, retrievers, some cross-breeds, Samoyeds, and Siberian huskies. Hounds, such as foxhounds and basset hounds, are also considered medium breeds. Labradoodles and cockapoos are two breeds suitable for people with allergies to dog hair.

- **large breeds (from 55 to 85 pounds)**
  German shepherds, standard poodles, Siberian huskies, Alaskan malamutes, American akitas, Japanese akitas, Pyrenean mountain dogs, Dobermanns, giant schnauzers, German short- and wire-haired pointers, and old English sheepdogs.

- **giant breeds (from 75 to 120 pounds)**
  Great Danes, Irish wolfhounds, Rottweilers, mastiffs, Newfoundlands, Bernese mountain dogs, and bull mastiffs.

Buying from a Breeder

If you choose to buy from a breeder, it is important to ask to see the parents. Are they registered? If they are not, ask why. Enquire as to the relationship of mother and father. If they are father and daughter or brother and sister, walk away.

If the breeder shows you photos instead of showing the parents, this may be cause for alarm as you can almost certainly say it is a puppy farm that may have puppies in every room. I went to a breeder 13 years ago, while working in animal welfare, and I got a collie pup. I was shown photos of a collie and German shepherd who were said to be the parents. I was shown all of the pups by the owner, who at the time did not know I worked in animal welfare. The pups were pure-bred collies. I returned the following day with my colleague and my suspicions were confirmed that the person was running a puppy farm. Between us, we removed over 120 pups from her home, not including the pup I had gotten the day before. Needless to say, the owner was prosecuted and then given a sentence of a year in prison, a fine of £5,000, and a lifetime ban on keeping animals.

If you buy from a puppy farm, when growing, the pup can have serious health issues, which my pup unfortunately had. Temperamental issues were also a concern. I love her all the same. She was temperamental where strangers we concerned and was very protective of me. Unfortunately she died before her 18th birthday.

I would advise anyone who is considering buying a dog to not buy from a breeder.

Why Rescue?

Rescuing an animal means you are giving the animal a second chance at life and the animal will give in return a life of unconditional love. Rescuing can also help ensure mass breeders will be eventually forced out of business.

A lot of breeders do what is known as interbreeding, which means breeding the father of the pups with a daughter and a mother with a son. They don't give you the full background and the reason if they are pure-bred and not registered they maybe interbred. This goes for a lot of uncouth breeders.

Rescue dogs are there for whatever unfortunate reasons. They are fully assessed, including temperament, before being put up for adoption. If they are assessed as unadoptable, then the centre has what are known as sponsor dogs. The reason they may be deemed unadoptable is they may have been traumatised, possibly ill-treated, or the owner may have died. There are all sorts of reasons.

I hope this will help you decide. My life has been made up of rescuing cats, dogs, etc., but it was the choice I made.

Illness and Infections to Watch Out For

Whether you decide to buy or rescue, there are illnesses and infections you will need to look out for in cats and dogs.

- *Blocked bladder.* In the case of dogs or cats not urinating, this will require immediate veterinary care as it can be fatal.
- *Ear mites* are a concern in cats. These are black. Immediate care is needed as the cat will constantly scratch at its ears and face, causing sores. If left untreated, some cats will also start to pull out their fur.
- *Canker* in dogs' ears will have a very strong odour and can be very painful. Immediate veterinary care is needed.
- *Cancer* in dogs and cats. Owners should regularly check for lumps as many can unfortunately be passed off as age lumps. It is important to have these checked.
- *Styes.* The eye area should be treated by a vet as styes will cause the animal to scratch and make the area bleed, which in turn can cause a more serious infection.
- *Bleeding.* If your cat or dog has been neutered and you notice any unusual bleeding similar to being in season, immediate veterinary care is needed as this can be a matter of life and death.
- *Parvovirus* will cause dogs to go off their food, vomit, and pass blood from the back passage. Parvo is treatable if caught early. You should seek immediate veterinary care. If left untreated, dogs can collapse and may die. Parvo is contagious and can be passed to other dogs.
- *Cat flu.* Cats will have symptoms, such as sticky eyes and runny nose, and will go off their food. This is contagious to other cats and, if left untreated, can be fatal. Veterinary care is essential.

Vaccinations

Vaccinations are essential in fighting the causes and spreading of diseases in cats and dogs.

Cats need to be vaccinated against feline flu and HIV, among other diseases. These require annual booster injections.

Dogs need a seven-in-one injection with annual boosters. In case of multiple-occupancy kennels, kennel cough vaccine is recommended. Kennel cough can be very distressing for dogs. If you are planning to board your dog while away, your dog will need to have an up-to-date kennel cough vaccine.

Taking Your Pet on Holidays

When you decide to travel abroad with your pet, there are a few things you will need to know.

- All cats and dogs need to have a valid pet passport, which you can obtain from your vet. A colour photo of the pet is optional. The maximum size is six centimetres by four centimetres and should show a clear image of colours and markings.
- A veterinary health certificate may be required.
- Ensure your cat or dog has been microchipped.
- Dogs will need to be up to date with all vaccines plus kennel cough and rabies before travelling.
- Cats will need to be up to date with vaccines and will require rabies shots over a certain age and leukaemia, especially if the cat is normally an outside cat.

Dogs and cats should ideally be acclimatised prior to travelling in a pet carrier. Five is the maximum number of animals allowed to travel with you. Consider the climate in your chosen destination. Remember your pet will be used to the climate and conditions of where you live, but if you are travelling to a hot or colder climate, you need to be prepared as they may struggle with the change. For a country where it is too hot and your pet might suffer with heat exhaustion or a country where it is cold, you will need to consider the length of the fur as they may not be able to cope.

If your pet has a medical condition which requires medication, you may want to bring medication with you. Talk to your vet. Don't forget to bring water for your pet.

Remembering these things will help make your trip abroad easier. Enjoy your journey.

The People Who Helped Me along the Way

I started this journey at just seven years of age. Through the years, I have met some people who have made the journey worthwhile. Thanks to Crispin and Mork, I met Marie Lusher, with whom I have a very good friendship. Groomer Janet Marie Adams has been like a sister to me and a wealth of information. She has been responsible for grooming all of my dogs over the years, which she has always done brilliantly. Janet has yet to meet Gillie, Tess, Bess, and Cleo. Laura Skelly has helped me along the way to becoming a professional dog groomer. Knowing these people has been of great benefit to me and my animals. Thank you.

Smokie and one of the tortoises

Millie 2 year old border collie
rescued from bad circumstances.

Stormy 1-year-old Rabbit

Tess Labrador x border collie 9 years old

Baby Horsefield Tortoises 4 months old

Kiara tortie cat 4 years old

Mork Siberian husky x German shepherd passed away aged 15 years and 4 months from cancer

Smokey Applehead
Chihuahua 6 years old

Harry Applehead Chihuahua
4 years old

My son with his cat

Ben Alaskan malamute rescued
from death row at 4 years old

Gillie pointer x springer spaniel
rescued from death row at 4 months

Sonny Siberian husky passed away
aged 14 years and 8 months

Jess welsh border collie passed away 3 days before her 8th birthday all because the vet could not do their job properly. Rescued from a puppy farm.

Printed in the United States
by Baker & Taylor Publisher Services